mnemonic

March 8, 2012   'raven in flight'   Jane Tims

mnemonic
soundscape and birdsong

poems & drawings by
Jane Spavold Tims

Chapel Street Editions

Appreciation of Place

Chapel Street Editions exists within the unceded and unsurrendered territories of the Wolastoqiyik, Mi'kmaq, and Peskotomuhkati people. The work we do is born from the stories carried by this land and its inhabitants. The animals, plants, soil, water, and air make this place home for the Indigenous people who belong to this land, for the descendants of those who took this land and made it a belonging, and for those who have since come from away. Chapel Street Editions holds a deep appreciation for our place within this land and the stories it tells. We honour the land's Indigenous caretakers and are grateful for their wisdom and guidance.

Published by
Chapel Street Editions
150 Chapel St. Woodstock, NB Canada E7M 1H4
chapelstreeteditions@gmail.com
www.chapelstreeteditions.com

ISBN 978-1-988299-53-2

Library and Archives Canada Cataloguing in Publication

Title: mnemonic : soundscape and birdsong / poems & drawings by Jane Spavold Tims.
Names: Tims, Jane Spavold, 1954- author.
Identifiers: Canadiana 20240283996 | ISBN 9781988299532 (softcover)
Subjects: LCGFT: Poetry.
Classification: LCC PS8639.I568 M64 2024 | DDC C811/.6—dc23

"Northern Parula" watercolour on the cover by Jane Spavold Tims

Author photo by Denis Beaudoin

Book design by Brendan Helmuth

Chapel Street Editions, Ltd. gratefully acknowledges the financial support of Arts Culture New Brunswick.

dedication

to my dad
who took us to Port Maitland
to find fool's gold
and listen to shorebirds

Table of Contents

Foreword

Jane Tims and I share interests in flora and fauna, especially birds and edible plants. Her knowledge of birdcalls and habits of specific species displayed in this book brought many sounds and images to mind. As a nature photographer, my task is easy compared to Jane's. What I see through a camera lens, she shares with us in her poems and drawings.

The natural world offers many hidden treasures to those who have the desire to explore. Jane is sharing more than drawings and poems with us; she is sharing precious moments, her special treasures.

Readers of this book will be encouraged to do their own exploration of the natural world and perhaps share their findings in creative ways like Jane. If you are an artist, like Jane, consider doing poems, drawings, and paintings. Consider photography or whatever creative form you like, perhaps song writing, singing or even dance. Like Jane, learn about what you see in nature and bring that to your creative endeavours. She has experienced wonderful moments connecting with nature and has beautifully described and illustrated them for us in this book.

She has made me hungry for an apple, cooked over a campfire.

Robert Shortall
Richibucto-Village, New Brunswick

a song across the water …

Jan 8, 2012   'two Mourning Doves'   © Jane Tims

drawing doves

grey sighs beneath graphite
or where eraser softens
troubled feathers

doves lament, disturb
fine detail, mourn
fingers tremble

pencil–strokes beak
and fingernails, kernels
of corn, husks of sunflower

three fates, spinning

1.

wound on the rock
mended by waterfall thread

2.

at last I touch
the water
real, wet water
      (not a report or diagram
      but the flavour feel and smell
      of water)

it pours through my fingers
delivers to me
mosses
lichens
      (the moth on the pin where she has always
      wanted to be)

3.

the doe must feel this
     as she crosses
     the road-to-nowhere
     when birch and aspen
     enfold her

or the ant
     as she maps the labyrinth
     on the rotting morel
     when she touches the ground
     (blessed ground)

or the needles of red pine
when they find the note
split the wind into song

singing glass

pond
       an arm drawn back
       from the river
smooth as a wetted stone
       discovered in the pebble
       clatter on the shore
       held in the curve of my hand

slate grey
cradled in the hillside
rim of river
       set spinning
       seven flat skips
       skim surface

       a flaw in time
       while stone
       slaps water

pond hardens
       chatter of stone
       on ice
       a single note
       across glass
       set ringing

over and over, return
to the shore
      to skip flat stones
      send a song
      across ice
      across water

Dec. 20, 2011   'Chickadee'   © Jane Tims

harvesting rose hips for the dye pot

berries are orange-red,
fewer than yesterday
chickadees sputter, tack
a syllable to their brisk mnemonic

boughs springy, possessive,
ready to lash with thorn
rose hips, broken string
of beads, scissor-shorn

end-blossoms are spiders, limber
thick-skinned berries
bob in a vat of rain
chickadees, upside-down

acrobats
in the brambles
black and white feathers,
brown wool

Jan. 5, 2012   'Hairy Woodpecker'   ©Jane Tims

kissing bridge

covered bridge, a resonance
chamber, timbre intensified
laughter, a car engine
the rumble of tires

vibration of boards, loosened
birdsong, nestbuilding
hammer-hollow of a woodpecker
patter of woodchips

breath, heartbeat, footfall
giggle, lips press and separate
a shout—*goodnight*
heading home for dinner

echoes gentle
bolts creak
timbers settle

grit of a blade
carves letters in wood
cleans bits of whittle
from the groove

engraver mutters
riff to a love song
a whisper, to rafters given
and amplified

Jan. 2, 2012   'Nuthatch'   © Jane Tims

morning bird chorus mnemonic

American robin
first grey light of morning
chirrup, cheerup, cheeree

mourning dove
oo-oo-hoooo

white-throated sparrow
oh dear Canada-Canada-Canada

black-throated green warbler
whee, whee, whee, wheezie

ovenbird
teacher, teacher, teacher

goldfinch
tweet-terreet-terreet-tereee

hermit thrush
flute-like, ethereal, each repetition a new pitch
close, then farther away

winter wren
impossible mnemonic, scribble bird

northern parula
whirrrr-zip
a glimpse where old man's beard lichen
hangs from the trees

an eastern Phoebe
nasal *fee-bee*, repeat
nest in the eaves

a red-breasted nuthatch
quank quank, yank yank
monotonous, bored bullfrog

black-capped chickadee
fee-bee, chick-a-dee-dee-dee

raven
auk auk, auk auk

woodland mnemonic

winter wren declares
its territorial rim, song
a scribble and a scrawl
joy, abandon, delirium

snipe winnows, pencils
an arc of sound, plays seek
and hide in the wet wood
dimensional courtship ritual

nuthatch, bored, pulls
endless rope, *yank, yank, yank*
hangs upside-down, beats
a seed against the shingles

parula flirts with colour
hides, flaunts its clever
whirrr-zip, only glimpse
a flutter of leaves

mourning dove

Zenaida macroura

wind wakens, descends stair
notices shadow, gaps
in cladding, the hollow
of the tower, slow breath
across mouth of bottle
amethyst, buried in sand

reed widened, a song
solemn, riff and echo,
distant train expands
across thin valley
a child hollows her hand
shapes lips for a kiss

tries to whistle, her breath
a sigh, a puff to cool
the chowder, still simmering
on the fire, thick and
needing stirring, onions

potatoes, corn, and
curdled cream, a woollen
shawl wrapped around, warmth
tightened to struggle,
viscous as lilac scent,
unable to breathe

hollow loon syllables …

gossip

cattle-corn rustles, brittle
whispers and secrets
murmurs and sighs
wind-syllables
and rumours
not a single
discernible
voice

campfire in winter

1.

campfire   inadequate
camp stool   uncomfortable
alderscape   unbeautiful

nevertheless kindling
in the knapsack is dry
   matches
yellow apples
wrapped in newsprint
   a knife

2.

you leave the fire   the starting and tending
to me   the preparation of sharpened sticks
impaling of apples

you swing the axe
hack at the alders

3.

apples acquire a layer of soot
flesh swells   skin splits
cider weeps on the fire sings the song
of tea at boil
I breathe sweet steam
and smoke

you bend to taste
sauce beneath the skin
smile at me
agree it is wonderful
turn away from the fire
hack at the alders

as usual   you have missed
the point
the lingering to talk   about nothing
in particular   to listen to the snow
sizzle beside the fire

I slide my teeth along the surface of the apple
rind slips like satin from the bed
I swallow the peel   ash and all
taste the discontinuity
where warmth meets
the cold
of the core

4.

face too hot
back too cold
eyes full of smoke

the trick is to concentrate on fire and keep
the chill from bone
pretend not to know
the moment will come

we fill the fire pit with snow
and black advances
on every side

5.

backpack empty
lungs exhale
trees parallel and grey

we trudge towards home
wounded by the quenching of fire

cornrows

at the first rustle
of shadow on skin
I wake
beside him

I slide from the bed
flip the latch
climb through the window
he will be angry
the thought
delights me

I cross to the cornfield
silken rows of ribbon
higher than my head
an army, khaki-clad
could march here
one row over
and we would all
have solitude

I shift rows
catch a glimpse
of tassels
chevrons
boot heels
click into the next row
ribbons quiver

takes nine minutes
to find a cornrow
north to south
leads back to the house

I cross the yard
pause on the threshold
      I hesitate
      a stranger

cornstalks whisper

I raise my fist
hammer on the door

imitating loons

1.

granite
scoured by ice
faint striations
etched by fingernails

2.

this misty distant place
you chose for quiet conversation
      muffles you
      sequesters me

your mouth moves
but it does not make sound
      you are telling me you still love me
      I think

I hear
      maniacal laughter of loons
      the chuckle of water

your lips synchronise
with hollow loon syllables
I smile a little
      you think I am remembering old times

I try to copy the loon's
      extended melancholy
      eager query
      come-hither titter
      quavering cry

my whistle is too thin and shrill
      you think I want a kiss

I never could copy that birders' loon call
with the breath
      and the cupped trembling hands

I do it now
the sound is a hiss
      you think my hands are cold
      try to hold them

3.

from a distance I watch him
      I envy his dive into anonymous water
      wish I could sink to my neck in the lake

4.

I am not good at imitation
so I make do
      uncomfortable giggle
      winnowing sigh

I edge a little closer to the water

hanging out bedding to dry

by the last acre
of oat field
grown golden in the sun
and wind

wet sheets billow
up
up and outward
the long husks of the grain heads
sigh like pebbles
sorted by the sea

pillowcases
pegged to a blue horizon
tug at the line
cedar masts are set
firm in the island till

quilts and coverlets
spinnaker and mizzen
carry me
over the wind-washed
waves of grain

glacial erratics

1.

on the outcrop
above the barren, acid lands
    two rafts of stone
    tilt
    back to back

sheltered
between them
    ashes of fire
    prototype of home

2.

I watch the water
    an ancient lake
    plugged with moss
you watch the wind
    waves of leatherleaf
    and lambkill
once we shared horizon

back to back
sometimes we speak
but words and meaning
are lost to wind
we feel only vibration of language

a lament beneath the howling
where breezes find a way
through cracks in the back door
and fissures in the wall

3.

each stubborn stone
protects its song

eerie music rises
unkempt harmony

the panic of butterfly flight…

yellow rattle

Rhinanthus minor L. synonym *R. crista-galli* (L.) *Hartm.*

roadside weeds
    tickle my ankles
    parchment whispers
        like Alberta prairie

rattler whirr
I freeze
    as I do when mouse feet patter
    in a house I thought empty

shake
loose seeds
in paper packets

    yellow rattle snouts
        test the air
    crista-galli flowers
        toothed as a cock's comb
    chatter at the north wind

claquette
    tap dance on the chilly breeze
sonnette
    quick scratching at summer's door

butterfly

scrap of paper
       plucked from my hand
                wind a tease
          always one wing beat
      beyond the finger tip
  attempts to read
its delicate code
      of dots
             and dashes

a yellow Post-it note
      folded on the tower
         of a blue sky cornflower
              a tatter
a musical note
      set to the panic
         of butterfly flight

      a curtsy and away
across the field

      pursued by a butterfly net

      and a killing jar

heartbeat

alive in morning   birdsong   thump thump thumping   slow
as a pulse   then faster   final beats too quick to count
a ruffed grouse   in the thicket
drums for a mate

all day I think of him
and smile

buried in evening   birdsong   a thud on the window
the grouse   sighs in the grass   tail narrowed
feathers ruffled at his neck   oddly bent
fingers on his throat   faint flutter
blood from his beak

I smooth him   into a mound of dead leaves   inspect
window   a feather sticks to the glass   moves
as though nostrils   draw faint breath

nothing broken

outfield quiet

ball field, neglected
corner of bottom land
in an elbow of river

these were the problems:
    busy road, no parking
    every spring – a flood
    tee-ball and juniors compete for field time
    batter up! and on-deck nine-year-olds
    are down there, dabbling
    in the river

decision made
bleachers
hauled away

up at the new field
cars honk, parents
shout advice

potato chips and hot dogs
pop in cans
lemonade

old field, quiet as an outfield
dark cliffs hover over bend in river
weeds and grasses tangle tall

a pileated woodpecker focuses his scarlet head
on a backstop post, staccato facsimile
of bat and ball connect

Nov. 23, 2011   'crows in trees'   Jane Tims

morning song

in the morning
dew soaks the grass
and Canada
belongs to the crows

croaking ravens
cawing crows
familiar, unheard
backdrop to Canadian dawn
    (theme music
    in Canadian film)

conversational rattle
discusses gold and letters

a two syllable scream
haunts the fields
    solitary sorrow
    throned at the top
    of a tamarack

black wings bruise the air
he calls an alarm
screams to his mate
    the love of his life
    with only the fall of the dew
        for an answer

silent is the shroud of black feathers
strung by the feet from a pole
beside a garden

where she braved the flapping man
and dared to pull new corn

in the morning, Canada
belongs to the crows

walk in the grey forest

this is unknown land
a place I have never seen
but dreamed
the sad dreams of wandering
where silence is fragile
snapped in two by a twig
or leaf-fall

I step carefully
disturbance no louder
than the exhalation of wind
the muttering of moths
between dying trees

this is ancient land
where I have not walked
fallen trunks and branches
draped with lichen
the burial place of the forest

something watches me
flattened to bole of maple
betrayed by rattle of beech leaves
or birch bark papers
shaking free of its leaf garment
rising from forest floor

I am an intruder
a desecrator of places
even a careful step
is hard on the hollow land

it will take time to learn to walk here
to find game trails
where scales of fir cones
have filled the hollows
to hear the words of the woodland
to know that dying trees
are not an omen
but part of the forest's life

hand-crafted

Picoides pubescens (downy woodpecker)

daft little bird
propped, pubescent, plump
  bang your silly
  head against the tree
      eat a bug

your sculptor used
deft fingers
  to point your beak
  solidify your tail
  paint feathers
      foam on black water
      snow on dark woods
      night sky with planets
      berry-stain
      your downy crown

May 19, 2016 'Ovenbird shuffling in leaves' Jane Tims

fear of heights

as dizzying to look up
in the forest
as down
into an abyss

trees taper so

they lean
water birch
against fir
rubbed raw
where branches touch
or reach for one another

and sudden, wrenching sounds
a branch swings back or breaks
loosed by a squirrel
burdened where crows complain

or where an ovenbird scolds
teacher teacher teacher

May 8, 2018   `Winter wren`

winter wren

Troglodytes hiemalis

how to find
centre of forest
joy, the objective

tiny tail
shivers as he sings
delirious trill

Troglodyte
darts into thickets
creeps into crevices

lifts an eyebrow
joins a chime of wrens
elusive ripple

varied trill
incoherent whir
tremble to warble

distinguish
the note, the half-note
the tone, the tangle

forget where
you once were going
indecisive
scribble bird

grown to lean on one another…

May 9, 2012   'American Black Duck'   Jane Tims

frog-croaking moon

(Mi'kmaq name for the May moon)

under the May moon
bullfrogs glub-grunk
underscore spring peeper trill

rasp of a black duck
rowing in the reeds

friction
of fir and maple
grown to lean on one-another

uncertain spring migration

if it rains
the night road
leads home
to lowlands
and hollows
      vernal pools
      north of the highway
swollen with rain

mists crawl
towards me
vignettes
sweep the windshield
      frogs cross the roadway
      follow ancestral memory
blurred by rain

some nights
the tail-lights ahead
are my only family
red streamers on wet pavement
      tadpoles from the egg mass
      grow legs
      absorb their tails
navigate the road

I watch
phone poles
potholes
hidden driveways
headlight echo on trees
      frogs flattened
      crushed on the pavement
mailboxes with uncertain names

centre line a zipper
seals left side
      to right
the coming home
with the leaving
      frogs plead
      from the wetlands
never saying goodbye

spring peeper mnemonic

eat cream of wheat —
ream of wheat —
creamy-wheat —
wheat cream

my wheat cream —
my creamy wheat —
eat wheat-e-cream —
wheat cream

sounds in the silence

1.

my children skip
round and around the well
around the rusty pump
the drive has been long
but they slept in the car
and now they are wanting
some water

I am a wish for sleep and silence
but they cannot hear
the click of my jaw
beneath their chanting

they think I am trying
to be silly
creaking the wooden handle
in desperation
(the pump has lost its prime)

2.

the mosses in the trough
are patient, they understand
how best to ask
they take the first drink

3.

spruce boughs
drape over me
roof of the kitchen sags
(only room of the old house
still standing)
spruce needles and shingles
are folds in the pink fists
of the setting sun
sky so rosy
it summons
improbable solitude

4.

beneath the din
I hear a parchment rattle
wings unbend
beneath the eaves
a cauldron of bats
stirs the twilight

I hear the tiger lily
close over
its glossy seed
the proud sigh of an owl
the horse chestnut
spreads her fingers
to protect green seed pods
spiked and sticky
snug in the tall grass

building homes

we fly kites
learn field and sky
set copper whirligigs to spin

      yellow flirt crosses blue sky
      potato-chip potato-chip potato-chip
      per-chick-or-ree

we build our cabin
with 2 by 4s, trusses and boards
spiral nails and woodscrews

      birch bark
      woven grass
      spider silk

you line our walls
with fiberglass, I quilt curtains
for our windows

      goldfinch waits while female tucks
      her nest with thistledown
      tufts of cattail, puffs of dandelion

Nov. 28, 2011   'Red-eyed Vireo'

54

red-eyed vireo

Vireo olivaceus

1.

olivaceous
outlaw
black-masked

2.

can't see you
can't find you
can hear you

where're you?
over there
where're you?
nowhere

3.

in November
birch bark tatters
of nest, ghost-thief
of summer

4.

gone now
what'd ya do?
did an answer finally
come to you?

drinks on the patio

the setting spins
on the river
golden while the mayflies dance
with gilded wings

this is conversation!
a cold glass
singing ice
white wicker
umbrella shade
hills wistful
beyond the gauze
of mayfly dancing

dazzled by the play of sun
and words on water
your voice
your smile
who cares what you are saying
as long as the lines are long
the tone is light
and mayflies stir
the air above the river

I listen
with a nod of my head
a flutter of my hand
the corners of my mouth lift
to smile

my ears and eyes
have better things to do

sunlight slides on cobwebs
spun across the river
our voices slur
while mayflies dance
the rise and fall
of their glass bodies
and your laughter

liquid on water

old man's beard

Usnea subfloridana Stirt.

you and I
years ago
     forced our way
     bent through a thicket
     of lichen and spruce

     Usnea
     caught in your beard
     and we laughed
         absurd!
         us with stooped backs
             and grey hair?

found a game trail
     a strawberry marsh
     wild berries
     crushed into sedge
         stained shirts
         lips
         and fingers

     strawberries
     dusted with sugar
     washed down with cold tea
     warmed by rum

today
an old woman
     alone
lost her way in the spruce
     found beard
     caught in the branches
and cried

pause to listen . . .

sand

1.

I still find grains
of sand in the tent
in seams and corners
       tinsel in summer
       snagged between floor boards

I sweep
grains scurry
into crevasses
       creep out when I am gone
       tangles in vacuum cleaner brushes

2.

today is hot and still
orange floods the tent
shadows, fir boughs and *Kalmia*
scratch at the canvas
       a partridge drums

I remember the blue
of glass and icicles
fir boughs, laurel
       and laughter

I remember the blue
of sea glass and sea breeze
gull cries
slick salt air
         sand pelting the fly

3.

tonight
my children will
drink cocoa
sing by the fire
beg another chapter
of the book we read
I will search for the flashlight
and the glint of tinsel
grit of sand
will trouble me

time on the shore

1.

spit of sand
grains in an hourglass
poured through gaps
in a cobble sea

2.

waves advance
try to tangle me
wash me, turn me
like a sea-smooth stone

but I know about tides
I move myself inland
each hour

3.

he watched whales blow here
saw sea horses dance
filled his pockets with sea glass
pitied the sandpiper
sprinkling tracks the waves erase

I hear the hiss of air
the echoing wail
small stallions prance on my toes

I close my eyes
forget to move

4.

he takes us prospecting
we wedge into crevasses
keen for pyrite gold
cube within cube
embedded in stone

we always forget the hammer
we chip and scratch with fingernails
reach across rock
dare the waves

5.

a sanderling cries
quit quit!

6.

shorebirds
befriend me

a dowitcher sews a seam with her bill
bastes salt water to shore

the sanderling shoos back the tide

terns
plunge into the ocean
and complain they are wet

May 19, 2016 `black-throated green in leafing maple` Jane Tims

fairy tale

she spins spleenwort and fern
weaves a scarf, celandine
     for her daughter
       to give her something brilliant
       to wear on darkest days

she spins bracken, weaves vine
between threads tucks the murmur
       of the black-throated green
       petals of flowers
       as good a lure as any

knows the secret, whispers
the name as she weaves
       as she spins
       Rumplestiltskin

might have told her a story
if a daughter would listen

crows too

crows burden the trees
gather their iron grits
criticize one another

they slip through gaps
in the matrix
and are gone

their wings are bruises
on the afternoon, their wind
is deliberate and desperate

hardened to the goal

grim women
in black
watch one-another

hide key
beneath doormat
and glide

towards the town

adolescent crows

1.

they hang out on branches
in the vicinity of home
too gawky for the nest
lack feathers to fly

they practice on the old parlour organ
(the one with a hole in the bellows)
the adolescent dirge -
bored variations
bid goodbye and beckon
to mama

2.

gaping of beaks
is instinctive
what's crammed in
or leaves
is hardly consequential

unsavory morsels
from the black delivery truck
do not fill gaps in the gullet
or gnawing in the craw
any more than tiresome
expulsion of air
reduces its size

3.

clamping of beaks
is also instinctive

when, curious,
I approach the witch's broom
(once served as home)

canny, quiet
adolescent crows
fall craving-quiet
branch
to
branch

no shivered twig
or creeper snap
echoes distant caw
of mama

4.

she inks circles on the sky
speaks to yearning ennui
explains why well-fed, hungry youth
should follow and leave
their mama

fiddleheads

thin music in the May-woods,
trowie tunes from the peerie folk,
a bridge between spring peepers
and the wind, fiddleheads carved
in Sensitive red, Ostrich green
the bow strung by spiders, riff
in the violin trembles
as potential uncoils, music
befuddled in a Cinnamon
web of wool

morning

        Tranton Covered Bridge

swallow twitter
lodges in the angles
of mortise and beam
folds back a corner on silence

bank beaver parts
a seam on the satin of river
sets free a feather storm
of birdsong

blackpoll warbler
curious in tumble
of alder branches
twee
and a red-wing
tow-ee

a stony path flows
beneath bridge
cattle, released to pasture
line up to drink

tree swallow

Hoyt Station Covered Bridge

twitter, liquid as water
simmers across floodplain
seeps and shallows

three circle swoop
three quick flaps
to climb and glide

white throat
blue-black wings
quick tuck into bridge

a twee and a flutter
a perch in eaves
rest and a short run

to ram inside boards
neither frightened
nor confused

its goal the blue-bottle fly
on the inside-shadow-side
of sun warm boards

sticky tongue, tail prop, zygodactyl feet

Mill Settlement Covered Bridge

morning chorus, chain of birdsong
(robin melodic, whitethroat mnemonic
wheezy phoebe, junco click)
grubs mumble, coil in rotting wood

beneath low woodwind, blazing brass and string
drum roll, jagged percussion
black jackhammer, downy woodpecker excavates
bridge soffit, sugar maple stump

beak throws wood chips, heaps sawdust, splinters
a grey smudge shudders, dapper black and white
bright head-bars, red blur, stammer-tap
steady stutter, busyspeak

summer song

Patrick Owens Covered Bridge

Sunbury County
sings in its sleep
           purple vetch
           hop clover
     bluegrass
at the roadside

hay in rows
           a staff
           empty of song
     waiting
round bales and their shadows
half notes for an oboe

honey bee
ditty in the pink
           old fashioned roses
           bid country roads
     enter the covered bridge
glimpses between planking
rock music on water
tires drumming loose boards

deer look up
cattle low in the meadow
     owl to whitethroat
        counterpoint
    lupins pepper the air
  rushes by the Rusagonis
north and south

big moon crescendo
     over Sunpoke
  firefly
follies in the fern

evidence of buffalo

"…in this field, years ago, I kept buffalo.…"
                                    farmer, selling his land

massive posts brace a page-wire fence
woven with grey birch
dusty wallows where soil is crushed
and only lichen will grow

three apple trees trodden
parallel to ground
eroded feed trough
strung together with nails

cedar waxwings search the fence
coarse hairs for their nests
winds nuzzle and whisper
through brush of pine

voices

night moth
lifted into fire
heart of a bird
trembles in its song
last flight path into
reflected wood
small voices in the walls
plead for a mouse mother
trapped and tangled

owl wisdom
from the mouth
of a dying oak
sap bleeds into pails
a spruce grows
as the chain saw sings
wraps its heart
in layers of wood
the children weep

a path to the door...

June 24, 2016   `thrush ethereal`   Jane Tims

hermit thrush

Catharus guttatus

neither visceral nor guttural, ethereal
tip-toe in tree tops
air pulled into taffy thread
a flute in the forest
froth on a wave

rain trembles on leaf tips
guttation drops on strawberry
a lifted curtain of mayflower

I saw you there
hidden in the thicket
and I followed

climb the ladder and sing
then step to the rung below
heads up, thoughts of the new day
parting of the beak
pulse at the throat

hairs lift
at the nape
of the neck, fingers
warble the keys
between middle and ring

catharsis

evening edge

evening edge
of lake
a corner torn
from the loaf
of hills
red with setting

faint click
sun gone
nasal chuckle
from far shore
dusk and bread crumbs
scattered on the water

arrows etched on glass
a glimpse of summer night
tucked under wings

blue-winged teal
eager for crust and crumbs

body language

threads cross the road
spin from ditches
fine hair lifted
from the shoulders, laid
across the eyes

black ice waits

this same wind
        stirs the surf
            at Torr Bay
        hurries me
            along the Diligent shore
        moves pillars of salt fog
            into Deep Cove

tonight, wind lurks
in ditches, disguised
as woven snow

my teeth clench
my right hand
grips the wheel

left hand
rests on my knee
open palm, face up

radio on for comfort
bare centre strip
snow-packed and slippery

Feb. 23, 2012   'male Purple Finch'   Jane Tims

purple finch

Haemorhous purpureus

sunflower seed and millet
purple finch posed on a branch of maple
      sullen brow
      blunt beak
      metallic tick

he knows my eye
at the edge of the glass
my struggle for stamina

he is immobile, dipped
in pomegranate, stuffed
with sunflower seed

he sees me sidle to the chair
sees me settle

still
as seedless husks
of sunflower

Nov. 29/2011   'Goldfinch'   © Jane Tims

goldfinches

Spinus tristis

feathers distil yellow
from atmosphere, cheerful
essence of sunflower

birds tipple, sip champagne
make small talk at parties
animated gestures

wilted scallops on air
the gregarious always
gather intelligence

best neighbourhood feeder
best seed
least squirrel

Feb. 25, 2012 'Pine Siskin' Jane Tims

watch-winding

Spinus pinus

listen for advance
of winter

siskins wait in trees
wheezy twitter

glance over-shoulders
fidget, alert

zreeeee, p–p–p–ree
vigilant

pine siskin
winds its watch

stepping stones

flakes descend, pause
on mittens, stack
against the wall
the long grey scarf
is a path to the door
in powdered snow
where, in summer
lily-of-the-valley crowds

the wool, dark
slate, grey dye from pips
boiled in spring, squeal
as we gather, the shrill
pipes of children
playing in snow
called inside, leaving only
shadows, boot prints
on stepping stones

pitfalls

soft places
hollows in the leaf layer
deadfalls to snag the surest ankle
roots to reach for a body
chasms to claim it

spaces to spill
sunlight, gaps in the grey
of pine, admit the riot of leaves
fit keys of maple into holes
in the layer of cloud

snags in the curtain
knots in the floorboards
eyes in the blackness of night
and whispers
flaws in the fabric, seams
to part and peer through

paths we have crossed before
in other ways

wood witch

burdened by snow
a tree tumbles a witch's broom
the witch set free

a hex on the snowpack
death rattle of a crow
slate where the dog runs
cuts her feet, soft rubies
in every track

a hex on the room
warm as I left
now cold

end of day

(after a painting by Andre Philibert 'Mon pays …
c'est l'hiver')

new-feathered, the valley
a black and white wing
stretches from horizon
the beat encloses
clouds and sky

field under snow, the back
of a settled dove, a lone
skier pressed towards
shelter, amber
streak of sky

Acknowledgements

Years ago, on a Canadian Nature Tours expedition to Grand Manan, as the botany tour guide, I found myself amazed by the dedication of the birders on the trip. Plants held still for observation, so I often found myself waiting patiently beside some woodland herb while those with binoculars chased an elusive warbler through the forest. Now, I am grateful to those dedicated birders, and to Peter Pearce and Owen Washburn, who encouraged me to listen with understanding to the morning chorus.

In the long winter months, our bird feeders show us we do not pass through the winter alone. Thanks to my husband Glen and my son Michael who have laughed with me over the antics of the birds and squirrels, deer and raccoons at our feeders. I am also grateful for their patient listening.

Many thanks to Alan Edgar (alan@science-music.karoo.co.uk) who put the words of 'hermit thrush' to music after a study of the bird's complex melody. 'Hermit Thrush Song' is the resulting musical arrangement. https://www.sheetmusicplus.com/title/hermit-thrush-song-soprano-with-pianoforte-digital-sheet-music/22120849. Many thanks also to Mary Lee McKenna for playing the 'Hermit Thrush Song' on the piano for me, to help me know Alan Edgar's melody.

Thanks also to the members of my writing groups, *Wolf Tree Writers* and *Fictional Friends*, who offered comments and support. And thanks to the readers at my blog www.janetims.com who give me a place to share my pencil drawings.

Thank you to Ann Gardner for use of her photo as the basis for the drawing "ovenbird shuffling in leaves."

Some of these poems have appeared elsewhere: *All Rights Reserved* ("body language"), *The Amethyst Review* ("hanging bedding to dry," "sounds in the silence"), *The Antigonish Review* ("cornrows," "the three fates, spinning"), *Canadian Stories* ("sand," "time on the shore"), *The Cormorant* ("morning song," "summer song"), *The Dalhousie Review* ("campfire in winter"), *The Fiddlehead* ("old man's beard," "yellow rattle"), *Green's Magazine* ("an uncertain spring migration," "singing glass"), *Pottersfield Portfolio* ("drinks on the patio"), and *Women & Environments International Magazine* ("crows too," published under the title "grim women"). Some of the poems have appeared on my blog at www.janetims.com. Three poems are from *in the shelter of the covered bridge* and one is from *within easy reach*.

The manuscript for *mnemonic* won the Alfred G. Bailey Prize in the Writers' Federation of New Brunswick 2016 Writing Competition. Some of the poems were written under Creation Grants provided by artsnb (the New Brunswick Arts Board).

About the Author

Jane Tims, a botanist, historian, writer and artist, was born and grew up in southern Alberta and now lives in rural New Brunswick. She obtained her B.Sc. and M.Sc. in biology at Dalhousie University and later a B.A. in anthropology and history at the University of New Brunswick. During her career, she worked in environmental protection in the fields of air quality, watershed management, and community planning.

She is a member of the Writers' Federation of New Brunswick (WFNB). In 2020 and 2022, she won Third Prizes in the WFNB Writing Competition for her poetry manuscripts, *a glimpse of sickle moon* and *perish, persist, escape*. In 2022, her book, *a glimpse of water fall*, was shortlisted for The Fiddlehead Poetry Book Prize in the New Brunswick Book Awards.

She has published seven books of poetry, including *within easy reach* (2016), *in the shelter of the covered bridge* (2017), and *niche* (2020). She has independently published twelve books in the *Meniscus* science fiction series and four books in the *Kaye Eliot Mystery* series.

In addition to writing poetry and fiction, Jane creates paintings and drawings of plants, birds, and landscapes. She illustrates her books. Her writing and art are all presented at janetims.com. Jane's main interests also include plant identification research, visiting New Brunswick's landscapes and the preservation of its built heritage.

www.ingramcontent.com/pod-product-compliance
Lightning Source LLC
Chambersburg PA
CBHW041146120626
46547CB00020B/3125